ATLANTA
BIRMINGHAM & ATLANTIC
MW00712039

Union City, Georgia, First activity for City Centennial Celebration. Sign in front of City Hall (100 years).

UNION CITY, GEORGIA

A PICTORIAL HISTORY

Celebrating 100 Years

by Marilyn Singleton McCain and Sally Summers Chapman

Cover photo: A picture of the Dixie Lake Country Club with pool and swimmers enjoying the water and sun. The dance hall is on the hill. Note the slide in the lake, and there were swings that went out over the swimming pool. There was also a golf course as part of the country club and a short-lived dog track. This facility was a very popular gathering place for people from all over, including Atlanta, and was considered the place to be. Mr. C. H. Gullatt owned and operated the Country Club. The dance hall building burned in 1931 and was not rebuilt. The pool was filled in, but for many years you could see some of the swing structures in the area. Mr. Gullatt operated this facility from the early 1920s until it burned in 1931.

The Donning Company Publishers
184 Business Park Drive, Suite 206
Virginia Beach, VA 23462

Steve Mull, General Manager
Barbara Buchanan, Office Manager
Wendy Nelson, Editor
Brueggenjohann/Reese, Inc., Graphic Designer
Derek Eley, Imaging Artist
Lori Kennedy, Project Research Coordinator
Scott Rule, Director of Marketing
Tonya Hannink, Marketing Coordinator

Bernie Walton, Project Director

Library of Congress Cataloging-in-Publication Data

McCain, Marilyn Singleton, 1952-
Union City, Georgia : a pictorial history : celebrating 100 years / by Marilyn Singleton McCain and Sally Summers Chapman.
p. cm.
ISBN 978-1-57864-500-8
1. Union City (Ga.)—History. 2. Union City (Ga.)—History—Pictorial works. I. Chapman, Sally Summers, 1938- II. Title.
F294.U6M38 2008
975.8'23—dc22
2008013485

Printed in the United States of America at Walsworth Publishing Company

UNION CITY, GEORGIA: A PICTORIAL HISTORY: CELEBRATING 100 YEARS

Table of Contents

UNION CITY

TO OUR FELLOW CITIZENS OF CAMPBELL COUNTY:

The Town of Union City takes this occasion to extend greetings to you.

We invite you to make your homes with us.

We invite you to establish your business with us.

You will find the people of Union City pulling together for the upbuilding of the Town and the County.

We are proud of our industries and of our citizens. You will find us truly glad to welcome you.

Union City products are known in almost every town and hamlet in the United States and in many foreign countries. The postal receipts at Union City are the largest in the United States of any town of its size. More than a million razors have been sold from Union City, going into 50,000 barber shops. The cabinet work manufactured at Union City is used exclusively by the Western Union Telegraph Company throughout the Southeast.

There is now under construction at Union City a Country Club that will be a big asset to Campbell County.

There has recently been established at Union City a wholesale flour and grain company.

Good schools are to be found throughout Campbell County, and we are especially proud of our school at Union City.

Vacant lots or residences may be purchased at reasonable prices.

You are invited to become one of us.

TOWN OF UNION CITY.

UNION CITY FLOUR & GRAIN CO.

Wholesale and Retail

To the people of Campbell and surrounding counties we call especial attention to the above-named firm, established by Mr. W. F. Lawrence and managed by Mr. C. J. Jeanes.

Mr. Lawrence has had 35 years experience in the flour and grain business. He will feature the line manufactured by the Acme Mills—recognized as the leader in the manufacture of feeds and flour. There is only one other mill in the United States that uses Cod-Liver Oil in the manufacture of their Poultry Mash Feeds.

Owing to the fact that over-head expenses will be low, the above company will sell these high-class feeds and the best patent flour at prices that will mean a big saving to the users.

(This advertisement paid for by the citizens of Union City, without the knowledge of Mr. Lawrence).

Welcome to Union City Newspaper Ad.

Foreword

What began some one hundred years ago as a thirty-acre farming and railroad community in Georgia is today the place we call "home." Founded on what was once part of Westbrook Crossing, Union City was no more than a little church and one or two farmhouses that lay partly in the piney woods and fields of then-Campbell County, Georgia. A writer who visited the place in those days wrote, "It appears to be a nice place for a picnic."

Shortly after the town was established, office buildings were built to house the Farmers Union and other industries the new town attracted. Its unique location contributed significantly to its rapid growth. It was on two railroads that gave outlet to every section of the country. It had the largest single-cylinder printing press in the South, an acidulating plant for manufacturing fertilizer, an implement company that manufactured all kinds of farm implements, a wholesale farm supply firm, a Union Bank, three hotels, and several razor companies.

Today, Union City is a community shaded by dogwoods, crepe myrtles, and Bradford pears, offering ready access to the busiest airport in the world, Hartsfield-Jackson International. It is a suburb that is just fifteen minutes from the "Gateway to the South," the city of Atlanta. Union City's greatest asset is her people, who are a diverse cross-section of citizens including skilled tradespeople, legal and medical professionals, educators, artists, small-business owners, and elected officials all caring for their community, their city, and each other. Union City, the "Progressive City," is a place where people have access to all the cultural, spiritual, educational, and economic opportunities of a large metropolitan city, but with the tranquility and charm of a small town. It is a place where one can find a real slice of America: a place to live in economic and racial diversity, and a place to call home.

Marilyn Singleton McCain

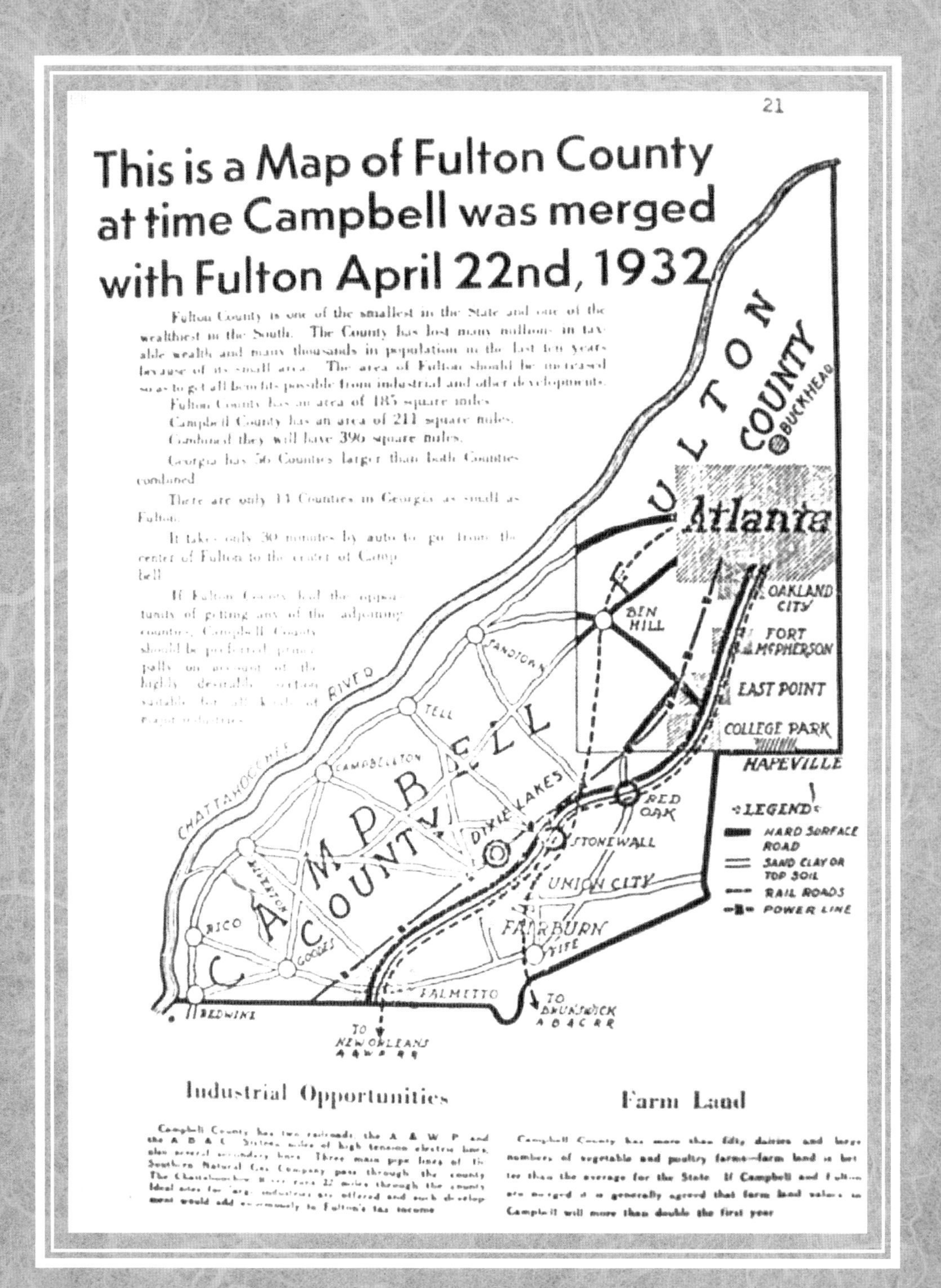

21

This is a Map of Fulton County at time Campbell was merged with Fulton April 22nd, 1932

Fulton County is one of the smallest in the State and one of the wealthiest in the South. The County has lost many millions in taxable wealth and many thousands in population in the last ten years because of its small area. The area of Fulton should be increased so as to get all benefits possible from industrial and other developments.

Fulton County has an area of 185 square miles.

Campbell County has an area of 211 square miles.

Combined they will have 396 square miles.

Georgia has 56 Counties larger than both Counties combined.

There are only 13 Counties in Georgia as small as Fulton.

It takes only 30 minutes by auto to go from the center of Fulton to the center of Campbell.

If Fulton County had the opportunity of getting any of the adjoining counties, Campbell County should be preferred principally on account of the highly desirable section suitable for all kinds of major industries.

Industrial Opportunities

Campbell County has two railroads, the A & W P and the A B & C. Sixteen miles of high tension electric lines, also several secondary lines. Three main pipe lines of the Southern Natural Gas Company pass through the county. The Chattahoochee River runs 22 miles through the county. Ideal sites for large industries are offered and such development would add enormously to Fulton's tax income.

Farm Land

Campbell County has more than fifty dairies and large numbers of vegetable and poultry farms—farm land is better than the average for the State. If Campbell and Fulton are merged it is generally agreed that farm land values in Campbell will more than double the first year.

Land map of Campbell County and Fulton County

FROM THE DESK OF THE MAYOR

Introduction

This year is very special for Union City, for we are now celebrating our hundredth birthday. One hundred years of keeping the promise of our founders to be the "Progressive City." One hundred years of ensuring that this community remains a place to call home for those born and raised here or those who sought Union City's charm and are now part of something special. What makes Union City that special place are the men and women who have contributed toward the betterment of this community by their relentless pursuit to raise Union City above all others. This community has always defined its character and its way of life by first understanding the elements and foundation of this City's history. From humble beginnings a hundred years ago, Union City has established itself as a quiet leader, not moved by the fireworks of larger cities or the daydreams of smaller communities. Our movement is paced by the talents and visions of people who understand that home is where the heart is, not our individual sense of grandeur and self-serving desire for importance.

As mayor, I am so very blessed to be a part of this place, at this time, for this purpose. Many of you should feel the same; you moved here for what Union City has to offer and not what it lacked. Union City is the quality of city that is sought after by many as their place of destination. We are the twenty-fifth fastest-growing city in the country and there is no mistake that the country is taking notice of what we are doing uniquely, rather than trying to be like others. Union City has never strived toward perfection, for perfection is unattainable. But Union City has had that uncanny knack to work toward the atmosphere of excellence, and while she is there she looks up and sees that there is more to her journey. She understands that her descent down can only be caused by her failure to catch the winds of her children's well-wishers and to soar even beyond her capabilities.

This publication will showcase that the journey of Union City is neither short-lived nor terminal, but that in her time traveled she has seen many things and will see many more. She has embraced those who loved her and has shunned those who wish to harm her. She understands the value of being the Hope diamond within the South Fulton tiara, but she also knows that the South Fulton tiara is more valuable as a crown of jewels. While many seek the warmth of her bosom, many need the courage of her protection.

In *Hebrews 10:1*, the scripture says, "For he looked for a city which hath foundations, whose builder and maker is God." Union City, you are certainly birthed by God's grace and sustained by His mercy. May God bless this city and most certainly the residents that call Union City home.

Thank You,
Ralph Moore

Official picture of Charlie S. Barrett as president of the National Farmers Union, circa 1907. Mr. Barrett had served as president of the State Farmers Union prior to becoming president of the National Union.

Chapter One

Union City was born as a result of the coming together of two individuals, Drewry Arthur Carmical and Charles Simon Barrett. Barrett was the newly elected president of the National Farmers Union at a time when the Union was looking for an appropriate location for its headquarters. Carmical not only agreed to provide the land for the Union headquarters, but he also offered to build a headquarters building that would accommodate some thirty offices to house the Farmers Union. Union City got its name because the Farmers Union headquarters was located here.

At the age of twenty-one, Drewry Carmical (sometimes spelled Carmichael) left Moreland, Georgia and came to Campbell County (now Fulton County) in January 1889 to seek his fortune. He would succeed beyond his wildest dreams. He found a good boarding place at the home of Mr. and Mrs. Westbrook in the Shadnor Baptist Church community. From the first, he was treated as a member of the Westbrook family; however, in October of 1889 he became a real member of the family when he won the heart and hand of Cora, the tenth of the eleven Westbrook children. The Westbrook family gave Drewry and Cora a thirty-acre tract of land from their farm as a wedding gift.

Drewry tried farming for ten years, from 1889 to 1899. His possessions never grew during this time, but he did gain some ideas from his farming experiences. He saw that better farm tools would help farmers of his day produce more. His brother Oliver had invented a combination fertilizer distributor and cotton planter that could be drawn by one mule. Drewry took over his brother's invention and improved the machine. Seeing the great need for improved agricultural implements, Drewry began inventing, improving, and manufacturing a new line of implements and wound up with a line of the best implements on the market.

The farm implement factory was set up in Fairburn, an adjoining community, and the Carmicals and their four children moved there in 1901. The factory prospered. Drewry received the highest award on all his machines at every fair he entered, and his machines became very popular in almost every state in the Cotton Belt. Sales increased, and Drewry's finances improved markedly.

In 1903, after the death of Mr. and Mrs. Westbrook, Drewry purchased their home and property and used that site as a farm until 1907. In that year, he persuaded the Atlanta, Birmingham, and Atlantic (AB&A) Railroad to run their tracks through his farm and

Drewry Arthur Carmical is in the center of this group of photos of the officials of the Farmers Union. (Mr. Carmical owned all the land where Union City started as a town.) Left to right: J. L. Barron; S. S. Barrett; B. J. Wootten; J. G. Eubanks

connect to the Atlanta and West Point (A&WP) Railway. The branch line of the railroad was to swing westward from Atlanta and then to turn south through what was then Campbell County. The city leaders of Fairburn wanted the new line to come through Fairburn, but Drewry offered the railroad free right-of-way through his property and got his neighbors to donate even more right-of-way. The railroad builders could not refuse the offer.

Drewry persuaded the AB&A railroad to build a junction track to the Atlanta and West Point railroad line and to place a passenger stop on Drewry's farm and at the Bethany Church in Fife, Georgia. Drewry got his railroad, together with a chance to build a new town on the old Westbrook home place.

The Farmers Union movement, and its goal to organize the farmers of the South, started in Texas in 1901. The movement quickly spread and an organizer for the union, Robert Franklin Duckworth, came to Union City in 1903. He was instrumental in getting Charles Simon Barrett of Atwater, Georgia, to help with the new organization. Barrett became president of the State Farmers Union and was later to serve as national president. He soon realized that his responsibilities made it necessary for him to travel extensively to all parts of the country. He also realized that, to accomplish such travel, he needed to be nearer to a railroad center with trains available to all parts of the country. When Drewry Carmical joined the Farmers Union movement, he proposed that the headquarters be set up closer to Atlanta and suggested the new railroad junction on his property as an ideal site. He offered other inducements, such as turning his implement factory over to the Farmers Union. The Union leaders agreed to come to the recommended site, so Drewry had the land surveyed in preparation for building the Union headquarters and homes for the Union officials.

As this project was coming together, Drewry realized that he had one of the most beautiful town sites in the South. A charter was drawn up for the new town and signed on August 17, 1908. A hotel was built and a bank was chartered. The post office of

Union City was established in 1907 and named for the Farmers Union. The Post Office Department did not approve the name because it was a two-word name, and, in their view, that would cause extra trouble in handling mail. Residents of the little community appealed to their U.S. Senator, Alexander S. Clay, who interceded—unsuccessfully—on their behalf with the Post Office Department.

Charles Barrett, the president of the Farmers Union, sought out Senator Clay and reportedly told him, "Senator, these fellows down in Georgia have a lot of faith in what you can do for them. Now we don't want to have to disappoint them, and we don't want to lose such a good Senator because of a disappointment." The Senator reportedly went at once to call upon President Theodore Roosevelt, his good friend, and explained the situation. There is not a full recording of that conversation, but President Roosevelt's closing remark has been quoted as something like this: "This looks like a matter of your political life or death, Senator, and I am not ready to lose such a good Senator. I shall authorize the Post Office Department at once to accept the name." From that day, the new town was called Union City.

Drewry Carmical became the first mayor of Union City. He was chairman of the town's school board, manager of the implement company, and, seemingly, had a hand in everything else that went on in Union City. For many years the Farmers Union thrived in Union City and the Carmicals did very well with real estate promotions. Drewry and Cora built a fancy new home on the site where the Westbrooks' home had stood for fifty years. It had white columns, marble steps, and many other adornments. Drewry also built a new brick church for the Methodist congregation.

But the days of prosperity were not to last. Support for the Farmers Union began to dwindle in Georgia with the coming in the mid-1920s of the boll weevil, an insect that attacked the cotton. (Prior to this time, cotton was "king" throughout the south. The boll weevil destroyed most of the crops, and to this day cotton farmers have to be careful when they harvest cotton. They can't leave any residue of the plants on the ground afterward, but must bury them to keep the boll weevil away. Many farmers turned to other crops after this period.) The Union Bank failed after an official absconded with the funds. As chief stockholder in the Union Bank, Drewry had to pay off the losses of others and to salvage what he could from his Union City estate. Much of his property in Union City had to be disposed of to settle his financial obligations. The Carmicals' fancy brick home was sold to Dr. and Mrs. A. J. Green, and for many years operated as the doctor's home and office. Today it is called Green Manor and is an upscale restaurant.

With what he could salvage, Drewry bought a farm in Madison, Georgia, and moved there in 1918. He later moved to Americus, Georgia, where he was able to revive his sales of farm implements—this time focusing on tractor-driven implements rather than mule-powered. Ultimately, he did recover financially, but he died in 1941 after a bout with the flu. Cora, his wife, died several years later. They are both buried in the Shadnor Baptist Church cemetery beside the Westbrook graves.

Charley Jeanes House. The Jeanes were early settlers in Union City.

Walter Cowart House, corner of Highway 29 and Dixie Lake Road, pictured in the 1970s. The house was built between 1908 and 1910.

Union City School—First Union City School, built in 1907 and located at end of present-day College Street.

1930—Charley Nixon's funeral at Shadnor Baptist Church, established in 1840 as New Hope. Sherman's troops camped in it and burned it in August 1864. The name was changed to Shadnor First Baptist in 1962. African Americans attended in the evenings in the 1870s and were baptized in a creek on Flat Shoals Road.

Electricity came to Union City about 1920. It was bought from Fairburn and was owned by three men: Walter Cowart, Dr. A. J. Green, and C. H. Gullatt. Later, ownership was sold to Georgia Power for six thousand dollars. The first sidewalks were paved about this time.

In the early 1920s, Union City became a resort town for wealthy families from Atlanta. Many elite families from Atlanta built summer homes on Dixie Lake, where there was also a dog track, golf course, and a swimming pool. In 1927, the Atlanta courts put the dog track out of business for gambling. Its building burned in 1931, and it was not rebuilt.

By the mid-1920s, membership in the Farmers Union shifted from cotton in the South to corn in the Midwest. Charles Barrett recognized this fact and announced in 1927 that he would not be a candidate for reelection as president of the Farmers Union. Following his retirement in1928, Barrett divided his time between working in Washington, D.C. (where he wrote a column, "Barrett Speaking," for the National Service Syndicate), and his home in Union City. He died in 1935 and is buried at Shadnor Baptist Church.

The Charles and Alma Barrett Family—Far left to right: Leland, Paul (with cats), Charlie, Howell, and Gaines (the baby). A sixth son, John, was born in 1911.

In 1932, Campbell County, an area of 211 square miles, was merged with Fulton County. Prior to the merger, Fulton had only 185 square miles and was the wealthiest county in the state. Even after the merger, there were fifty-six counties in the state larger than Fulton County, but the added territory did give Fulton considerably more room for industrial and business expansion. C. H. Gullatt, who had been Campbell County's representative in the state legislature since 1924, engineered the merger. This was the first merger of counties in the history of the United States.

J. H. Harris, an early developer of the town, conceived the idea of building a streetcar line, using a vehicle with a gasoline engine, which ran on rails. The original plan was to build the line from Fairburn to College Park; however, when Harris asked the leaders of the Fairburn community to help with its construction, they hesitated. Harris told them that without their cooperation, the line would run only from College Park and would stop in Union City. Fairburn then decided to join in the enterprise also. The "Dummy Line," as it was called, was a great help to the farmers and working people who had to travel to Atlanta. The line is presently MARTA, a bus line that goes all the way to Palmetto now.

Shadnor Baptist Church dates back to May 11, 1840. It was first called New Hope Church, but its name was changed to Shadnor around 1853, reportedly for a Mr. Shadnor who had done a lot of work for the church. The original church was built of logs, and it was located about where the Westbrook cemetery lots are now. Family names in the early church were Westbrook, Crumbia, Walker, Ritcherson, Jeanes, Mims, and Meeks. The log building was destroyed during the Civil War, but the church continued. In July 1897, W. H. Westbrook deeded one acre of land to Shadnor for a new building, and his funeral was the first one held in the new building. Shadnor bought almost three more acres of land from Mr. Carmical between 1905 and 1907, and Shadnor built a modern brick church building.

H. C. Emory was the first minister of the Methodist Church. Until Mr. Carmical built their church, the members met upstairs over the Union Cotton Grading School. Charter members in that church included family names of Barrett, Braswell, Carmical, Foster, Hendrix, Patton, Pierce, and Young.

In 1909, a weekly Prayer Band Meeting was started in a house along the AB&A Railroad in Union City. Several months later, the Prayer Band moved to another house located on what was then called Sugar Hill. The late Reverend Silas Moore served as the leader of these services. In the year 1911, being led by the spirit of God, this group of Christians was led

Carmical/Green House built between 1908 and 1910. Presently an upscale restaurant called Green Manor.

(Above) Charles Barrett House on present-day Watson Street. This is his second house; the first home burned.

to organize a church in the name of Jesus Christ, thus, Union Grove Baptist Church was officially organized. Reverend Walter Banks served as the first pastor of the church for two years. In 1911, Reverend William Tucker was called to serve as pastor for one year and he was succeeded by the return of Reverend Banks. Reverend Banks was recalled and served until 1914. The church continued to grow and eventually moved from Sugar Hill to the community called Graves Alley.

Some employees of the Farmers Union were members of the Church of Christ in Union City. They met in homes until the first church building was constructed on Roosevelt Highway in 1928. In 1935, a brick building was erected next to the older building. The first members included the family names of Drake, Goodson, Guilpin, Duckworth, Henry, and Joiner.

The first school in Union City was above a wooden store building. All grades there were taught by Miss Mertie Smith. Later, a two-story building was erected on College Street for pupils of all ages to attend. Mr. Jessie Smith was the first principal and Mrs. Ruby Foster was his assistant. Vera Carmical and others from this area taught school there. After the merger with Fulton County in 1932, all the high school children were bused to Fairburn. In 1940, a new grade school was built on Dixie Lake Road, where the land was given by C. H. Gullatt. In the 1970s, C. H. Gullatt Elementary School, named for businessman C.H. Gullatt, was built on Dodson Drive to accommodate the influx of new residents from the Shannon communities.

The first doctors in Union City were Dr. Hurd and Dr. Miles, and its first dentist was Dr. Marrow. Later, Dr. J. J. Wadkins practiced here, and he was followed by Dr. A. J. Green, who practiced here for many years.

Union City's factories were to go out of business and the town was to be at a virtual standstill for many years. In the early 1970s, Union City began to experience a surge of new growth, beginning with the Shannon community as a planned development of eight hundred acres, which includes a shopping mall of one million square feet, Shannon Villas, Shannon Glen, Old Virginia, Old Savannah, and Windham Creek. There has been a steady growth in single-family residences, condominiums, apartments, office parks, and low-density commercial sites. Beginning in the late 1990s, a strip of automobile dealerships was added along Highway 138.

The South Fulton Municipal Regional Jail, constructed in the late 1990s, is the first regional correctional facility in Georgia to be based on cooperation between cities (Union City and Palmetto) rather than between counties. The facility houses prisoners from the two cooperating cities as well as, by contract, from other Georgia cities and counties and from the U.S. Marshal's Service. The Regional Jail and the Union City

Railroad depot that sat on the Atlanta and West Point railroad and was subsequently moved to Union Street for the Woman's Club.

Drake/Weaver House located on Westbrook Place.

Justice Center were built at the same time, and the jail was uniquely constructed in a way that connects that facility by tunnel to the Justice Center's police headquarters, court system, 911 Center, and related city services.

In 2006, the Union City Planning Commission embarked on an ambitious venture of land acquisitions made possible by the introduction of Senate Bill 552 in the Georgia Legislature. The intent of the bill was to establish the charter for the new City of South Fulton and to permit south Fulton municipalities to annex adjoining land. Though the City of South Fulton did not come into being, Union City was able to nearly double its land mass with the annexation of 5,330 acres of property to the west of the city. This annexation brings the total area of Union City to 10,827.10 acres, and planning for this newly acquired area will include residential, commercial, and industrial development to further enhance the planned, forward-looking growth of Union City.

Written by: Marilyn Singleton McCain
Edited by: Dr. Robert Croom

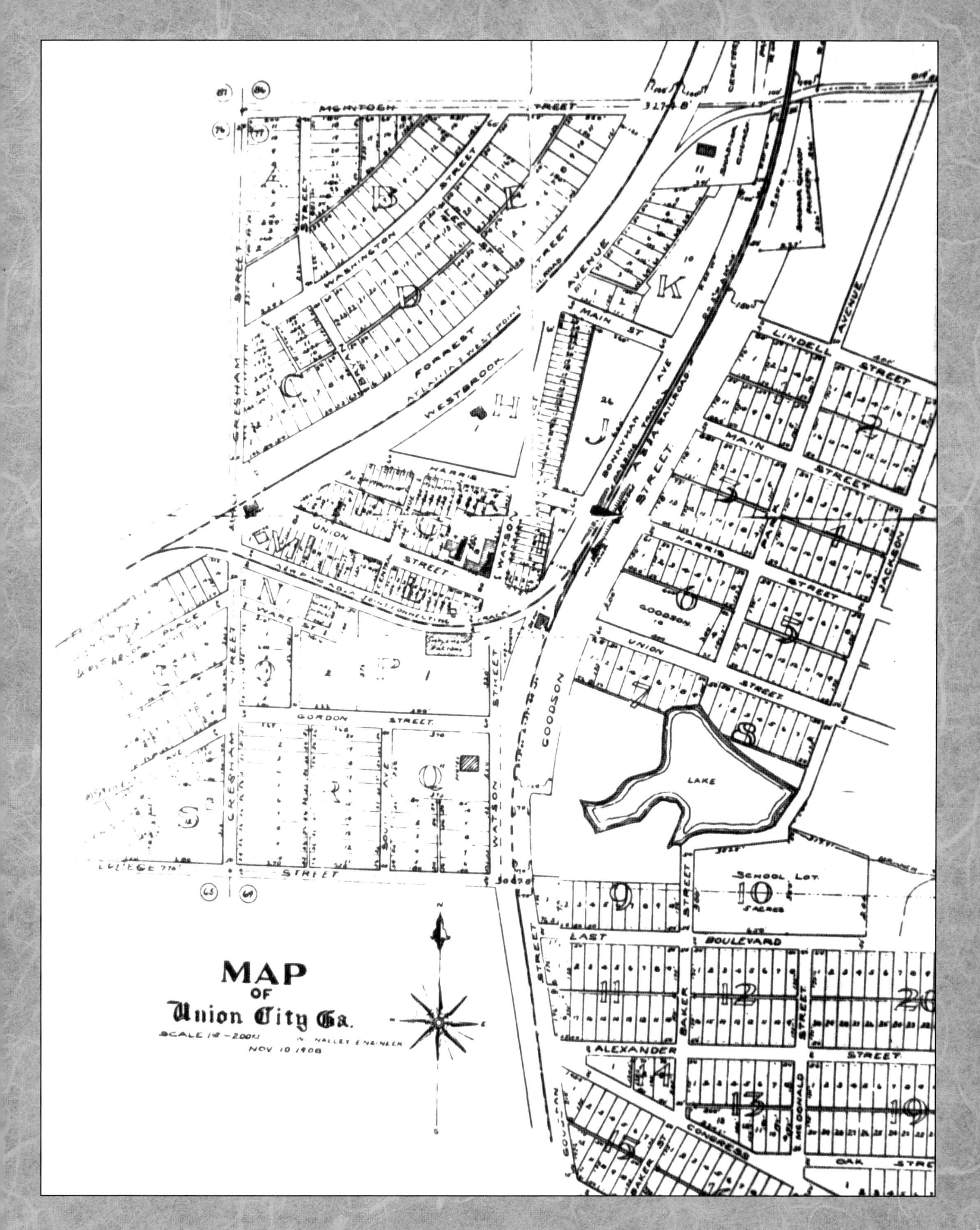

Plat of Union City, 1908.

J. O. Yarbrough Family (Mr. Yarbrough was the second mayor of Union City). Bernard A. Yarbrough, his son, is the little boy and he also served as a mayor of Union City.

THE FARMERS UNION COMES TO TOWN—1908–1917

Chapter Two

The first decade of the existence of the town of Union City, Georgia, was a very busy time because there was a big building boom going on. Mr. Charles S. Barrett moved to the town from Upson County to head up the national headquarters for the Farmers Union. Mr. D. A. Carmical had his land laid out in lots, which he sold or gave away.

New residents came to Union City to work for the newly relocated National Farmers Union and many of the other businesses. A two-story brick building was built in the downtown district, and it housed the Farmers Union, a telephone exchange, a bank, and a grocery store. There were lumberyards, a back band factory, two brick companies, a dry goods store, three hotels, several razor companies, a farm implement company, a fertilizer company, and a cotton grading school.

Mr. C. H. Gullatt was the first in Union City to open a razor distribution company, the Dixie Razor Company, and this was followed by many others, including Union City Cutlery Company (owned by Mr. Cowart); Middlebrooks Razor Company (owned by Mr. Middlebrooks); and National Manufacturing Company (owner unknown). They did not manufacture the razors in Union City but distributed them by mail order to barbers all across the country.

The city park and lake provided recreation for all the town folk and those from surrounding areas. The city park and lake were located east of the downtown business district between Union and College Streets. There were swings and slides that went out over the lake and a picnic area that was very popular. According to Sally Summers Chapman, it was an ideal location for city functions like dances and other social events. The greyhound dog track was located nearby, and was, for a short time, a venue for gambling.

The Fairburn and Atlanta Railway and Electric Car "Dummy Car" ran between the Atlanta and West Point (A&WP) railroad and U.S. Highway 29, and was operational from 1911 to 1921. The Masons held their "possum" supper in the school building, which was sponsored by Charles Barrett.

Shadnor Baptist Church (originally New Hope) had been a strong influence on the community since 1840, even though Sherman's men had destroyed the building in 1864. (The Church was renamed Shadnor First Baptist in 1962.). The United Methodist Church was formed and met in the Union Cotton Grading School until the church building was constructed around 1916.

Union City Population, 1910: 534

George Eubanks, bookkeeper for the Farmers Union, in his office. Mr. Eubanks also served as master of Union City Masonic Lodge.

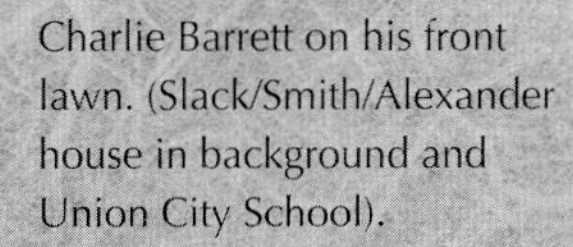

Charlie Barrett on his front lawn. (Slack/Smith/Alexander house in background and Union City School).

A group of ladies at the City Lake—1914

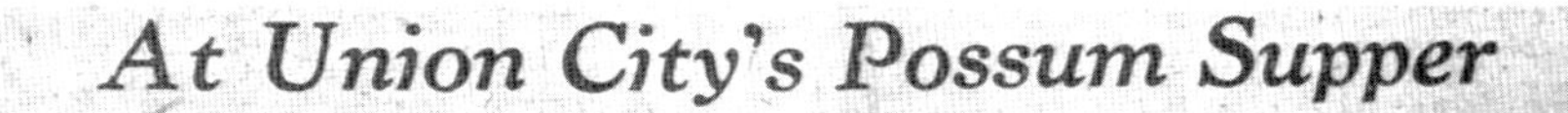
At Union City's Possum Supper

Larger picture shows guests at the possum supper given at Union City Thursday night in celebration of the institution of the new Masonic lodge. President Charles S. Barrett of the National Farmers union, a principal worker for the lodge and its opening, is seated at the left. Lower picture shows the men and women who prepared the feast of possum and 'taters and other Georgia delicacies.

Possum Supper circa 1910—Legendary Masons' "possum" supper held at Union City School, hosted by Charlie Barrett.

Farm implements of the Farm Implement Manufacturing Company.

A group outside the downtown business buildings.

Mr. J. T. Braswell's grocery store—1908. The Braswells were early settlers of Union City.

Peters Family—early settlers in the area. Only one in the family married.

The "Dummy" Car. A gasoline-powered trolley that ran from Fairburn to College Park. It was locally owned by stockholders under the name "Fairburn and Atlanta Railway and Electric Company," although there was no electricity. The "Dummy" trolley ran on tracks between the railroad and Highway 29. Circa 1917.

Business District—First brick building in Union City. This building burned in 1919 and was later rebuilt as a one-story building. Note the Cotton Exchange building in the background on right, which later became to be known as the Dixie Building.

Gates Brothers Lumber Company, with Duffey Hotel in right background and the Golightly/Whelchel/Robinson house in left background. Also note the top of train depot. This building faced Gresham Street.

Union Grove Baptist Church began as a weekly prayer band in a house in Sugar Hill in 1909. Rev. Silas Moore served as leader. In 1911, this group of Christians organized the church of Union Grove Baptist Church. The church eventually moved from Sugar Hill to Graves Alley.

Union City Methodist Church. The first building was built by Mr. D. A. Carmical. Before the building was completed, church was held upstairs in the Cotton Grading School building.

Misses Lillie Belle Drake and Edith Eubanks swimming at Dixie Lake. Circa 1924.

UNION CITY BECOMES A RESORT—1918–1927

Chapter Three

During this decade, even though the town was still growing, it faced much adversity. In 1919, the two-story business building burned. The hotels had burned in earlier years. The business district was rebuilt as a one-story building group.

The town folk took time once a year and "shut down" the town in August to enjoy an "annual watermelon cutting" at the City Park. This may have been a birthday celebration for the city. Oyster suppers were held in the Dixie building on Friday nights. The razor companies were continuing to distribute razors to barbers by mail order.

Dixie Lake Park/Resort was an attraction for many people from all over who enjoyed the pool, golf course, dance hall, and a short-lived dog track. The dog track was put out of business by the courts because of gambling.

The Union City Flower and Needlework Club was formed in 1924 and later became the Union City Woman's Club (see more about this in Chapter 9.)

The church building for the Church of Christ was being built. Members were meeting in members' homes.

Electric lights came to the city in 1925 thanks to a group of men, Mr. Walter Cowart, Dr. A. J. Green, and Mr. C. H. Gullatt, who bought the franchise and sold it to Georgia Power Company in 1926. City sidewalks were built from the profits of the sale.

Mr. C. S. Barrrett announced in 1927 that he would not seek reelection to the presidency of the Farmers Union.

Young ladies at Walter Cowart's private swimming pool.

Men and Greyhound dogs at the Irving (Ellena) Thompson home on Highway 29. These dogs raced at the dog track at Dixie Lake.

Union City School (grades one through eleven), showing the wing, which housed the first grade in the basement.

Homer Gullatt, owner of Dixie Lake Country Club and Dixie Manufacturing Company, with Lillie Belle Drake and "Uncle Alex." Circa 1920.

The annual watermelon cutting/picnic at the City Park/Lake—1919. Pictured are Misses Marion Veale, Nina Nixon, and Ruth Mason.

Miss Lillie Belle Drake's sixth birthday party. During an interview for this book, Miss Lillie Belle identified without hesitation all the people who attended the birthday party. They are, from left to right: first row—Ed Martin Green and Lillie Belle Drake; second row—Gene Russell, Edith Eubanks, and Frances Cowart.

Several men showing old car and buggy.

First Walter Cowart family. Left to right: Frances, Emily, Elizabeth, Fannie, and Walter. Mrs. Fannie Cowart was killed by a train at Westbrook Crossing in 1927.

Boys at Union City School on College Street.

A picture of the Dixie Lake Country Club with pool and swimmers enjoying the water and sun. The dance hall is on the hill. Note the slide in the lake, and there were swings that went out over the swimming pool. There was also a golf course as part of the country club and a short-lived dog track. This facility was a very popular gathering place for people from all over, including Atlanta, and was considered the place to be. Mr. C. H. Gullatt owned and operated the Country Club. The dance hall building burned in 1931 and was not rebuilt. The pool was filled in, but for many years you could see some of the swing structures in the area. Mr. Gullatt operated this facility from the early 1920s until it burned in 1931.

Graduating Exercise

Union City High School

Wednesday Evening, 8:30

PROGRAMME

1. Invocation ---------- Rev. Clarence Teurnan
2. Song ---------- Class
3. Address of Welcome ---------- Georgia Meek
4. Class Picture ---------- Idoleane Yarbrough
5. Piano Solo ---------- Addie Ree Patton
6. Class Poem ---------- Nina Nixon
7. Oration ---------- Jacob Patton
8. Piano Solo ---------- Nina Nixon
9. Class Prophecy ---------- Lillie Mae Yarbrough
10. Essay ---------- Addie Ree Patton
11. Piano Trio ------ Nina Nixon, Ruby Hogan, Addie Ree Patton
12. Class Will ---------- Ruth Mason
13. Valedictory ---------- Ruby Hogan
14. Literary Address ---------- Hon. M. L. Brittain
15. Delivery of Diplomas ---------- Prof. J. J. Brock
16. Song—"Farewell" ---------- Class

Union City High School Graduation Program—1918.

1918

The Senior Class

of

Union City High

School

requests your presence at the

Commencement Exercises

Wednesday, June Twelfth

at eight o'clock

School Auditorium

Class Motto:

Tonight we launch, where shall we anchor?

Class Colors:
Pink and Green.

Class Flower:
Pink Carnation.

Class Roll:

ADDIE REE PATTON
GEORGIA NELL MEEK
RUBY HOGAN
NINA NIXON
LILLIE MAE YARBROUGH
IDOLEANE YARBROUGH
RUTH MASON
JACOB PATTON

J. J. Brock, Superintendent.

Union City High School Graduation Program—1918.

Old Campbell County Marker located at the last Campbell County Court House, Fairburn, Georgia.

CAMPBELL COUNTY MERGES WITH FULTON COUNTY—1928–1937

Chapter 4

Fulton County was one of the smallest counties in the state and one of the wealthiest in the South. The county had lost many millions in taxable wealth and many thousands in population in the last ten years because of its small area. The area of Fulton could be increased so as to get all benefits possible from industrial and other developments. Fulton County had an area of 185 square miles and Campbell County had an area of 211 square miles. Combined, they would have 396 square miles. Georgia has fifty counties larger than both counties combined. It takes only thirty minutes by auto to go from the center of Fulton to the center of Campbell. If Fulton County had the opportunity of combining with any of the adjoining counties, Campbell County was the preferred choice, primarily because of its size as well as its proximity to the railroad line. This section became known as South Fulton County. Milton County (North Fulton) also merged with Fulton at this time. The county seat remained in Atlanta, as it already was the county seat for Fulton County.

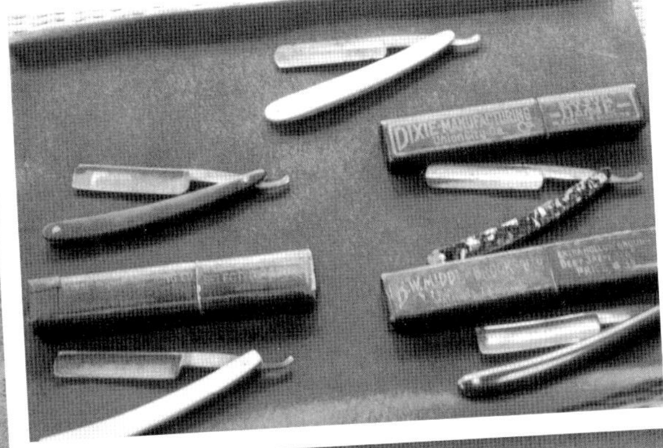

Dixie Manufacturing (letter head), owned by C. H. Gullatt. Dixie Manufacturing shipped straight razors to barbers.

Picture of razors distributed by companies in Union City. They were Dixie Manufacturing Company; Union City Cutlery Company, National Manufacturing Company, and Middlebrooks.

New picture of old furniture/casket-making company/Estes Manufacturing company (harness factory)

Union City Woman's Club members: Mrs. Irving Thompson, Mrs. Paul Barrett, and Mrs. J. T. Braswell. Circa 1935.

Railroad depot on the AB&A/AB&C railroad. Mr. Lee Grimes, believed to be the black man who carried mail to the railroad tracks for the post office. He would hang it on a hook and the trains would come by and grab the bag.

Grady Cook's Store, inside view. Located on Highway 29 at Westbrook Crossing. The people pictured are believed to be Grady and Ruby Cook with their son Donald, circa late 1930s.

First grade at Union City Elementary School 1932–1933. Miss Martha Harris is the teacher.

Group of girls with Estes Manufacturing building in background. Estes manufactured back bands for horses. The building also contained a casket and furniture-making company.

Cowart's Lake on Dixie Lake Drive—1943. Shadnor Church baptized members in this lake.

Union City Woman's Club "Tacky" Party—1935. 1) Mrs. Paul Smith; 2) Mrs. Lula Moats; 3) Mrs. Sudie Fowler; 4) Mrs. Tom Wages; 5) Mrs. Hollin Collins; 6) Mrs. Paul Barrett; 7) Mrs. Lem Drake; 8) Mrs. J. T. Braswell; 9) Mrs. Aubrey Jeanes; 10) Georgia Cowart; 11) Mrs. Walter Cowart; 12) Mrs. Lewis Camp; and 13) Miss Della Hopkins.

Marion "Bo" Cochran—Soldier in World War II. Cochran received a Distinguished Cross medal.

WAR TIMES—1938–1947

Chapter Five

By the 1930s, money was scarce because of the Depression, so people did what they could to make their lives happy. Movies were hot, and parlor games and board games were popular. People gathered around radios to listen to the Yankees. Young people danced to the big bands. Franklin Roosevelt influenced Americans with his Fireside Chats. The golden age of the mystery novel continued as people escaped into books, reading writers like Agatha Christie, Dashiell Hammett, and Raymond Chandler. During the Great Depression, the American dream had become a nightmare. What was once the land of opportunity was now the land of desperation. What was once the land of hope and optimism had become the land of despair. The American people were questioning all the maxims on which they had based their lives—democracy, capitalism, and individualism.

According to Sally Summers Chapman, "Union City had quite a few men and women who served during World War II. Times were hard as jobs were hard to find. The women (along with my mother) folded bandages for the Red Cross. Also, we had what were called blackouts—when the police siren sounded at night we had to turn all the lights out in case it was a true air raid. (Some people even said planes would drop fliers of some sort, but I don't remember that). I am sure there were some Union City casualties of the war but I can't think of any and don't know where there would be a record of this. After the war, the economy seemed to get better (at least it did for us.) It seemed that jobs were more plentiful. I think the population stayed about the same."

Union City Population, 1940: 884

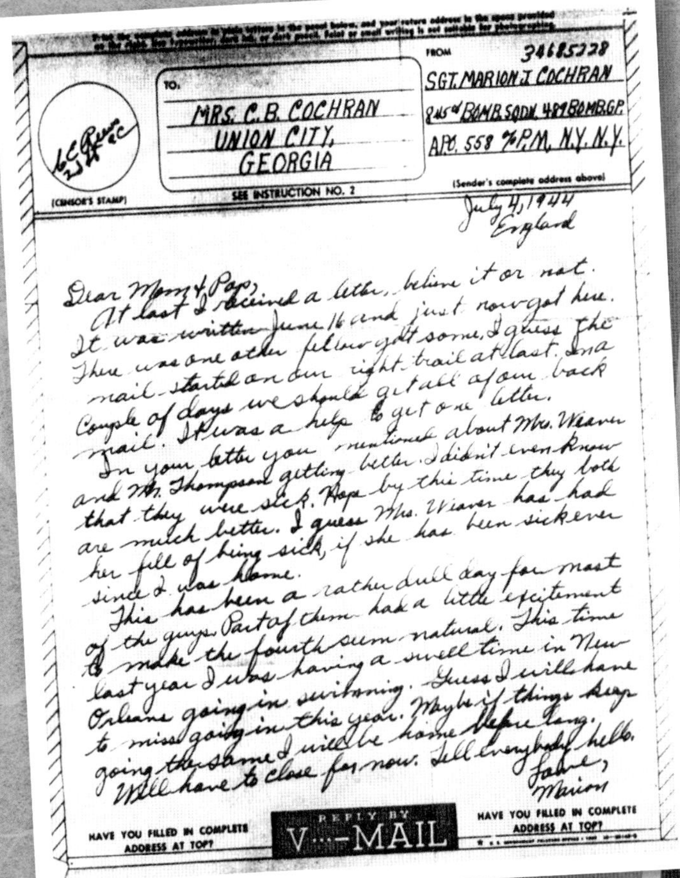

FROM 34685228
SGT. MARION J. COCHRAN
845th BOMB. SQDN. 489 BOMB. GP.
APO. 558 % P.M. N.Y. N.Y.
(Sender's complete address above)

TO:
MRS. C.B. COCHRAN
UNION CITY,
GEORGIA

(CENSOR'S STAMP)

SEE INSTRUCTION NO. 2

July 4, 1944
England

Dear Mom & Pop,
At last I received a letter, believe it or not.
It was written June 16 and just now got here.
There was one other fellow got some, I guess the
mail started on our right trail at last. In a
couple of days we should get all of our back
mail. It was a help to get one letter.
In your letter you mentioned about Mrs. Weaver
and Mr. Thompson getting better. I didn't even know
that they were sick. Hope by this time they both
are much better. I guess Mrs. Weaver has had
her fill of being sick, if she has been sick ever
since I was home.
This has been a rather dull day for most
of the guys. Part of them had a little excitement
to make the fourth seem natural. This time
last year I was having a swell time in New
Orleans going in swimming. Guess I will have
to miss going in this year. Maybe if things keep
going the same I will be home before long.
Will have to close for now. Tell everybody hello.
Love,
Marion

HAVE YOU FILLED IN COMPLETE ADDRESS AT TOP?

REPLY BY V...–MAIL

HAVE YOU FILLED IN COMPLETE ADDRESS AT TOP?

Letter from England, 1944—Marion Cochran to his parents in Union City.

Frances Cowart in her WAC Uniform during World War II, 1945.

Second Walter Cowart family, 1940s. Left to right: Walter, Jane, Georgia, Juanita, and Mary.

W. J. Lewis, grocery owner, with his son Tim. Mr. Lewis also served as a volunteer fireman.

1938 Shadnor Easter Sunday school group.

Frances Whittelsey at her home on Gresham Street.

Summers Children—Tommy, Sally, Eugene (Bunky)—in about 1939, with the Mann house in background. The Mann house faced Union Street. The house burned in the mid-1940s.

Dr. & Mrs. Albert J. Green on their twenty-fifth wedding anniversary in 1941. Dr. and Mrs. (Johnnie Hobgood) Green moved into the Carmical house in 1916. Dr. Green delivered many babies in Union City and surrounding areas. He had an emergency treatment room in the house with his office.

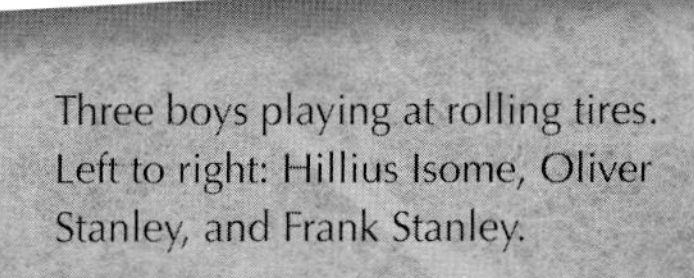

Three boys playing at rolling tires. Left to right: Hillius Isome, Oliver Stanley, and Frank Stanley.

Polly Miller on Lower Dixie Lake Road.

POST WAR—1948–1957

Chapter Six

As the nation demobilized, President Harry S. Truman faced a political battle. A one-time courthouse politician who owed his political success to the Democratic political machine of Kansas City, Truman had been a liberal senator and loyal New Dealer. Assertive and self-confident, he capably assumed the presidency after Roosevelt's death at the end of World War II. Congress rejected Truman's efforts to improve civil rights for African Americans. In 1948, Truman integrated the armed forces by an executive order.

During these years, Union City's economy was better, with more jobs available, and some houses were built during this time.

Union City possibly on corner of Gresham (west) & Hwy 29.

Union City Population, 1950: 1,490

Union City "New" School on Dixie Lake Road. This school opened in 1941.

Tommy Summers "firing" the pot belly stove in the Woman's Club Building (old depot).

Shadnor Baptist Church deacons 1952.

Edna Yarbrough, U.S. Marine. Circa 1950.

Eugene "Bunky" Summers in Air Force uniform, Korean War. Circa 1949–1950.

Catherine Foster and unidentified man.

Shadnor Church—First brick building.

Cotton grading school/Dixie/ Masonic building.

S. T. Foster

Union Grove Sunday School

CIVIL RIGHTS MOVEMENT—1958–1967

Chapter Seven

Thoughts from the Civil Rights Movement—the first totally integrated classrooms—from the Union City perspective, by Mike Isome:

There were a total of thirteen black students chosen to attend M. D. Collins in that first year, all of whom lived in the same neighborhood as defined by the Seaboard Coastline railway, Flat Shoals Road, and East Jonesboro Road. Some of us were related, but we all shared an even closer bond as we were considered the 1969 experiment—thirteen black students being bussed into a school of some twenty-five hundred students. None of us could have been prepared for the experience.

Marshall White, Michael Isome, Milton Foster, Manda Foster, Millicent Carol Wright, Patricia Williams, Milton White, Ralph Isome, Anna Wright, Robert Howard, Vicky Tinsley, Charles Lovelace, and Richard Williams—these were the thirteen who started the school year of 1969–1970 and represented the first totally integrated high school classes from Union City. Our bus stop was located at the intersection of Park Street and Flat Shoals Road. Consequently, ours was the last stop that the bus made on its way to the M. D. Collins/ Lakeshore campus. I remember as we gathered on that first morning we were all terrified of what we were about to face.

The bus finally rolled to a stop, and as we prepared to board, the bus was already about half filled with students from the large subdivisions northeast of Union City along Flat Shoals Road. These were all-white subdivisions of Pine Tree and Pointer Ridge in unincorporated Fulton County. There were a few more students thrown into the mix from pockets along Flat Shoals Road. As we stepped on to the bus we immediately noticed that every seat on the bus had at least one student seated, with items stacked alongside each. There were lunch pails, books, jackets—anything that would fill up the seat beside the students so that there would be no room left for any of us to sit. It was apparent that our fellow students had drawn a line in the sand. They did not intend to share seats with the experiment students.

Union City Population, 1960: 2,118

Union Grove Usher Board

Marshall White and I were the two larger and elder males in the experiment and the younger guys and girls were looking at us to see what we would do. Not a word was spoken as Marshall and I looked at each other and stepped into the middle of a moment. We walked down the center aisle and began pushing items aside from the seats to make room for our friends and family members. Most were afraid to sit but followed our lead, and eventually everybody was sitting down. Of course, some of the white students got up from their seats and retreated to other parts of the bus. Essentially, we succeeded in segregating the integrated bus in about sixty seconds, and our journey began. Most of us never realized the significance of what had just happened until the following morning.

Obviously, the incident had sparked some response on the part of school officials. The experiment needed to succeed without violent confrontation or incident. The following morning there was no need to repeat the actions from the previous day. We boarded the bus to find all of our white fellow students seated two and three abreast, with plenty of room for the experiment to sit. We also noticed that our bus was being escorted front and rear by APD/Fulton County Patrol cars. The escorts continued for only a few days and there were very few incidents related to integrating the bus.

Christian City: A City Within a City

Nestled on a five-hundred-acre campus among stately pines and pleasant walkways, sits a beacon of light to many…Christian City. Located in Union City, with the humble motto of "Loving people…loving people" Christian City reaches out to young and old and those in-between by providing safe homes to abandoned and abused children, affordable housing to seniors on limited income, and professional care to those in need of assisted living, nursing, and rehabilitation for Alzheimer's disease and other forms of dementia. Additionally, Christian City is a well-respected community for active retirees. Seniors can live out their latter years in a secure neighborhood setting with opportunities to participate in fun activities, make new friends, attend worship, do their banking, socialize, and get involved helping others through volunteer work. Christian City is affectionately referred to as a "City within a City" because of all the conveniences it offers and the strong sense of community that the residents feel.

It all started around a kitchen table. Back in the early 1960s, Ms. Millard Price was looking for a way to provide a safe place for homeless children. She met with her minister at Southwest Christian church, Jim Dyer, who agreed that this was a worthy endeavor and a calling from God. Others began to get involved and share the vision, especially members from numerous independent Christian churches throughout Georgia and beyond. Ms. Price offered to bear the cost of the first cottage, and Dr. and Mrs. Byron Harper, Jr., central participants in the visionary team, offered to donate the first fifty acres. The dream was becoming a reality, and the mission was clear: To minister to the needs of families with particular emphasis on children, the aged, and the infirm, by providing residential, health, and social services in accordance with the principles of the Christian faith.

The first of eight cottages opened on Valentine's Day in 1965 with eight little boys. Full-time house parents provide a nurturing family environment complete with sit-down dinners, household responsibilities, and traditions that create a sense of belonging. The funds to provide this care are raised through individuals, civic and professional groups, corporate sponsors, and the faith community, along with some support from the Department of Family and Children's Services. Over the past forty-three years, Christian City has been "home" to more than one thousand abandoned, abused, and neglected children. Licensed for up to sixty-four children, Christian City also provides foster care placement with well-qualified Christian families.

A few years following completion of the Home for Children, construction began on hundreds of patio homes for active seniors, followed by nearly three hundred apartments for seniors on limited incomes. As the needs of the residents continued to grow, so did Christian City! It was a natural progression to begin construction of an assisted living facility, a skilled nursing facility and rehabilitation center, and eventually a full continuum of care for the aging all on one campus.

At Christian City, the "future is now" and the needs of many are at our doorstep. A brand new state-of- the-art Children's Village will be completed this summer. When the original children's cottages are vacated, they will be renovated to make room for a new ministry for developmentally disabled "adult" children.

Over the past forty-three years, Christian City's campus has grown from fifty acres down a quiet country road, to five hundred acres bustling with life and filled with hope for more than one thousand residents. The dreamers keep dreaming…and God keeps providing.

Christian City is a nonprofit, nondenominational organization. For more information, please visit the website at www.christiancity.org or call 770-703-2636.

Vesta Drake at her home on Highway 29, with snow on the ground

All-volunteer Fire Department—1962. This group fought fires from Union City north to College Park, to the west, and Palmetto.

Officer Capus Isome, first black police officer. Rear: Police Cadet Albert Thornton, 1970.

SUNphoto by Kathy Jennings

Local forester retires

Louie F. Deaton, Georgia's first "urban forester," retired recently. Deaton became Georgia's first urban forester and among the first in the country in 1962 when he was assigned to Fulton County. In his years of helping the people of South Fulton plant and nurture their trees, Deaton has been recognized with many

Mr. Louie Deaton, a Georgia Forestry Commission forester in the local area. Mr. Deaton also served with the Union City Volunteer Fire Department.

Christian City/
Children's Home

Shadnor First Baptist
Church—remodeled

Shadnor First Baptist
Church Cemetery

Mr. Charlie Drake, curator of the Sequoyah Indian Museum.

THE SHANNON COMMUNITY COMES TO UNION CITY—1968–1977

Chapter Eight

The area that was to be Shannon Mall was covered with very large boulders. Some say it was a part of the natural granite fault line that extended from Stone Mountain and throughout all of South Fulton County. It took several years to blast them all. Residents experienced daily power outages as a result of all the blasting. Construction of the Mall began in the early 1980s. Shannon Mall opened around 1982. This description dates from the 1970s:

"Shannon is a new focal point for Metro Atlanta. Located at the intersection of Interstate 85 and Georgia Highway 138, just south of Interstate 285. Shannon is a total planned community of eight hundred acres consisting of a one-million-square-foot shopping mall, several thousand condominiums, apartments, office parks, and low-density commercial sites.

The Shannon Community will include a number of highly selective office park locations of both the single-story garden and the clustered high-rise variety. Shannon is becoming an important office center due to the convenience of its location to major traffic arteries, Atlanta International Airport, and a favorable labor market.

Other residential communities in Union City are the communities of Wellington Estates subdivision, Littleton Woods subdivision, and the community surrounding Dixie Lake."

Union City Population, 1970: 3,031

Sequoyah Indian Museum on Highway 29. Owned by Mr. Charlie Drake.

Shadnor First Baptist Church

Union City Trading Post—Formerly Garage of Berkel Buffington

C. H. Gullatt Elementary School—1996. School was named for prominent Union City resident and Georgia State Representative for Campbell County, C. Homer Gullatt.

Shannon Villas—condominium complex and first gated community.

Old Virginia—A condominium complex.

Old Savannah—A condominium complex.

Shannon Glen, a community of single-family, California-style patio homes.

Shannon Mall

SHANNON MALL INDUSTRY AGE—1977–1987

Chapter Nine

Shannon Mall will be the showcase for merchandising not only for Atlanta but also the Southeast, with four major department stores and one hundred shops on eighty-three acres. One of the nation's leading shopping center architects designed Shannon Mall with special emphasis on visual interest and solid marketing appeal "Totally enclosed with year-round comfort conditioning," Shannon Mall will feature a central courtyard with an ice-skating rink. Parking on all four sides will also provide extra shopping convenience. As a major regional shopping complex, Shannon will draw customers from throughout the Southeast but will have as its trade area the burgeoning population of 409,000 (by 1975), with average annual family income of $12,900. This includes Southside Atlanta, Union City, Fairburn, Palmetto, College Park, Riverdale, Jonesboro, Fayetteville, Peachtree City, Newnan, and the new city of Shenandoah, as well as Fayette, Coweta, Douglas, Carroll, and South Fulton counties.

Union City Population, 1970: 4,780

The Union City, Georgia, Train Depots

The Atlanta and West Point (A&WP) Railroad built the train depot in 1908 beside the railroad at the Gresham Street Crossing. It was used as a train depot until 1937. There was also a second building that was on the south side of the crossing, which was probably used for freight storage. Union City's outgoing mail was placed in heavy bags and hung up on hooks beside the railroad tracks. The trains would come along and a hook or device on the train would grab the mailbag. Mailbags for the incoming mail were thrown from the trains and a carrier would pick the bags up and carry them to the post office in downtown. This method of mail handling was used for many years after the depots were no longer in use.

The depot served as a railroad station for the travels and shipping of the National Farmers Union officials and other industries of the town. This was a common-type depot, and was twenty-five by seventy-five feet in dimension with "white" and "colored" waiting rooms. The railroad agent's office was between the two waiting rooms. There was a large room for freight and express shipments.

Railroad business at Union City dropped to almost nothing after the Farmers Union moved its headquarters in the late 1920s and early 1930s. Eventually, the railroad decided to sell the building and have it moved from the right-of-way.

The Union City Woman's Club, formerly the Flower and Needlework Club, had been searching for a building in which to hold their meetings and other functions. Meetings had been held in members' homes since 1924. Mr. Walter Cowart, husband of Mrs. Mary Cowart, a club member, was aware of the need for a club building. Since he was in the real estate business at the time, he became aware that the railroad company was going to sell the depot building. Mr. Cowart purchased the building for the club with one hundred dollars of his own funds. Through money-raising suppers, etc., the club repaid Mr. Cowart the hundred dollars.

Mayor Etris cutting ribbon for new Community Building, P.H. "Doc" Houston and Barbara Bohannon looking on.

The Union City officials provided the space on Union Street between Central Avenue and the City Hall for the building. The Fulton County Public Works Department moved the building the two hundred yards and took care of the placement of the building at its new home without charge.

In time, the Woman's Club renovated the depot for their monthly meetings and other uses. They installed a kitchen and restroom in the former railroad agent's office space. The floors were also refinished and chandeliers were hung. At this time, the building was heated by a potbelly stove that burned coal. The Woman's Club would rent the clubhouse out for functions, such as parties, wedding receptions, etc. The club members were certainly proud of their new building and rightly so as it was a pretty building!

New Railroad Depot/Community Building

The club rented out a small room to various people from time to time. There once was a beauty shop and then a barbershop in the small room at the end of the building. One of the Atlanta newspapers rented a room for distribution of newspapers at one time. In 1945, the City of Union City rented a room for use as a City Hall for five dollars per month. City court was held in the large room. It was in this room that Councilman P. H. "Doc" Houston was sworn in as police chief in 1945. Mr. "Doc" Houston served as police chief for many years and later served as a mayor.

The Woman's Club sold the building to Union City in the late 1980s for ten dollars, with the understanding that they could hold their meetings in it the second Wednesday of every month. Due to dwindling and aging membership of the Union City Woman's Club, the club was disbanded in the early 1990s. The building had been known as the Union City Woman's Club building from 1937 until the time when they sold it.

After purchasing the building, the city received a federal grant of four hundred thousand dollars to renovate the building again for a senior citizen's center. The outside of the depot was restored to its original state and modifications were made to the interior. The Archives Room is constructed completely of original wood from the building. About ninety to ninety-five percent of the windowpanes are original. Also, at this time Central Avenue was closed off and the building was moved westward and turned to face the City Hall where it is located now. In addition, a grant was received from the Fulton County Arts Council. The purpose of the grant was to have a mural painted depicting the life and times of the town when it started. This mural is hanging in the community house. The depot served as a community center for senior citizens until 2002 and serves as a city community center at this time. This is a historic building that the citizens of Union City should be proud of.

The second train depot was located on the Atlanta-Birmingham-Atlantic (AB&A) Railroad and was built about the same time as the A&WP depot. The first AB&A train ran through Union City in 1907. This depot was a common-type building also. With the decrease of railroad business in Union City, the depot was torn down years ago. A little farther north of this depot was the wooden water tank from which steam engine trains would stop to take in water. The water for this tank was drawn from the nearby city lake. This facility was also torn down years ago.

—**Sally Summers Chapman**

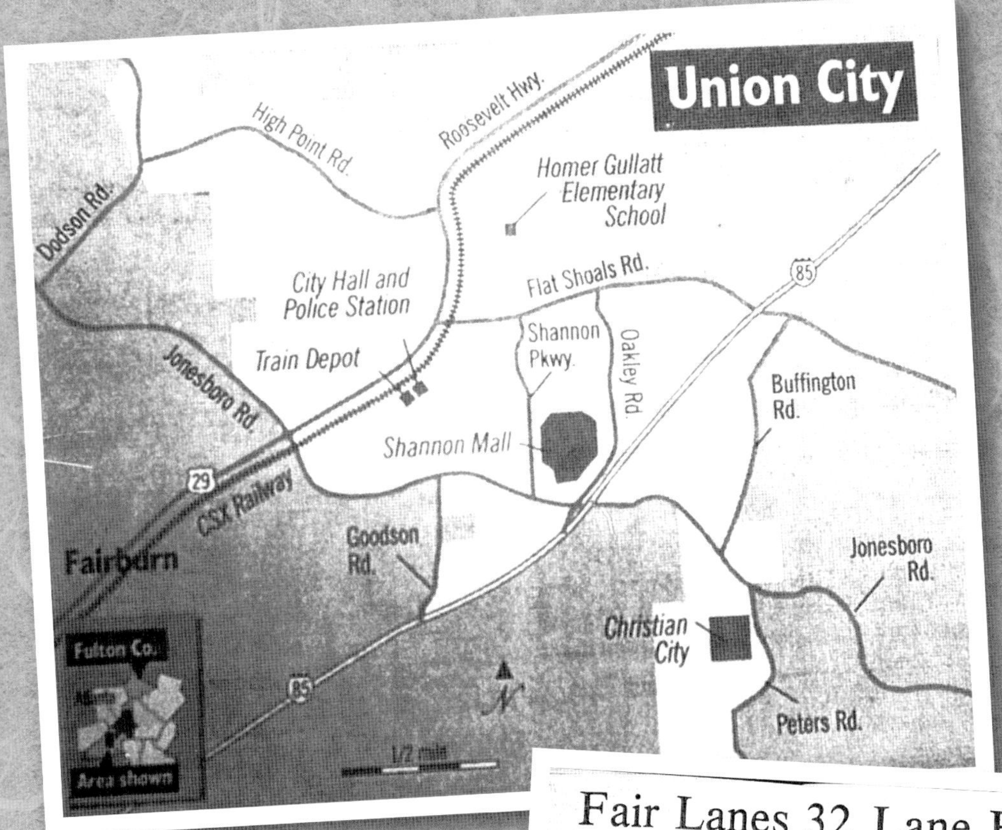

Land map of Shannon Mall.

Fair Lanes Bowling Center, newest bowling center in Atlanta, located near Shannon Mall. The thirty-two-lane family recreation center is located west of Shannon Mall.

Second fire station #2 on Shannon Parkway

Snow of 1982—Seven-year-old Jamie McCain builds a snowman.

New City Hall, built in 1985, with water tank in background.

Shannon Glen covered in snow.

Melear's BBQ, circa 1986 during their forty-year celebration. The Melear family ran the barbecue business from 1946–1996.

Walk up/drive up pay phone in front of Robinson's Antiques on Highway 29. The back band factory building is in the background.

Aerial view of Shannon Mall

Ribbon cutting ceremony for Shanon Mall.

Public Servants Elected and Appointed—1988–1997

Mike Isome, first African American police chief of Union City, joined the police department in 1977, and was promoted to sergeant in 1980. He transferred into the Criminal Investigations Unit in 1984. He became deputy chief of police and in 1995 was promoted to chief of police until the end of 2007.

Ralph Moore, Union City's first African American mayor, elected in 1994, has faithfully served the community for thirteen years, with wife Camilla at his side. Mr. Moore's training and expertise in urban planning and public administration has helped shape a different Union City in meeting the ever-increasing demands of an exploding and evolving Atlanta metro area.

Edith Elaine Bridges, first African American female police officer and dispatcher

Ronald Bridges, first African American city councilman.

Marilyn Singleton McCain joined the planning commission and was its first African American member.

Odell Mashburn, public servant. Served on city council, 1964–1989, and served on housing authority, appeals board, and currently on zoning board.

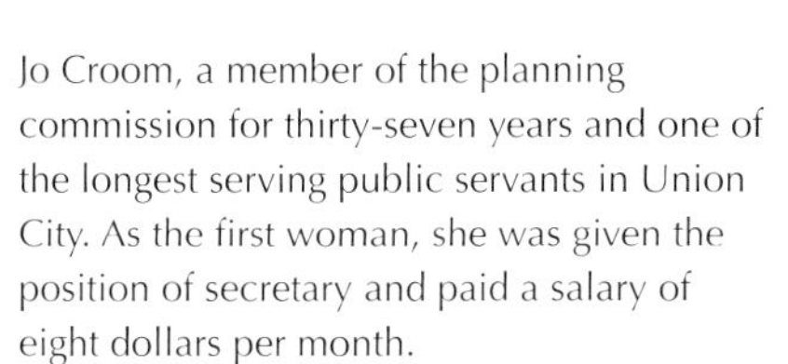

Jo Croom, a member of the planning commission for thirty-seven years and one of the longest serving public servants in Union City. As the first woman, she was given the position of secretary and paid a salary of eight dollars per month.

Helen Turner, first African American woman on the city council, served on the Union City Zoning Board of Appeals from 1990 until she was elected to the council in 1998. Since that time, she has served as a council member continually.

Ann Lippmann, first city planner. With the new growth explosion, the City of Union City hired its very first planning director.

Milton Foster, longtime resident of Union City. Twice ran for city council, currently serving on zoning board of appeals.

Jaki Cossey, the first African American city clerk of Union City

Current city council first row, left to right: Shirley Jackson, Mayor Moore, Angelette Mealing. Second row, left to right: Brian Jones, Vince Williams.

UNION CITY TODAY—THE PROGRESSIVE CITY

Chapter Ten

This decade has seen Union City trying to live up to its name as the "Progressive City". A struggling Shannon Mall got a new owner, an architectural firm did a livable centers study, a college came to town, and Union City struggled to find ways to provide its own water and sewer. With commercial development happening in surrounding cities, mayor and council seek ways to assist in the revitalization of Shannon Mall in the hopes of giving Union City an economic boost.

UNION CITY AWARDED LCI PLANNING GRANT

Union City was among three recipients in South Fulton to receive a sixty-thousand-dollar planning grant from the Livable Centers Initiative (LCI). Union City selected the community design and architecture firm of Tunnell-Spangler-Walsh & Associates of Atlanta to take its plan into action. They were picked from three finalists out of six proposals submitted and have already begun work by reviewing existing Union City projects and inventorying land use and analysis.

Union City will be eligible to receive significantly more money for implementation of their study through the federally funded program, administered through the Atlanta Regional Commission (ARC).

Tunnell-Spangler-Walsh has extensive experience in Atlanta and the Southeast. One of the projects that most appealed to Union City officials is the firm's work on the Winter Park (Florida) Mall Redevelopment, partnering with the firm of Glatting Jackson, who will again team with Tunnell-Spangler-Walsh in Union City. Winter Park was challenged by a five-hundred-thousand-square-foot mall that was badly in need of reinvestment. The team worked with both the city and the property owner to develop an alternative urban design concept that essentially integrated the city into the mall. Today, Winter Park Village is a revitalized "live, work, and play" community that is highly successful.

"We are looking for the help of the Tunnell-Spangler-Walsh team to remake the Shannon Mall area and environs into a seamless community," said Mayor Ralph Moore, himself a professional city planner. "With our enviable location on Interstate 85 and its direct

Union City Population, 2000: 11,621

Mayors' Park

connection with Hartsfield Atlanta International Airport and the amenities of Atlanta nearby, Union City has a very good chance of being a highly desired address."

Thomas H. Walsh, a principal of the firm, says he is very excited at this opportunity to work with Union City. "We've done a lot of work in Atlanta and her suburbs but the potential of Union City has really gotten our interest. We're grateful to have the opportunity to help Union City's vision and virtually recreate the downtown to this dynamic area around Shannon Mall."

City administrator Alan Grindstaff and city planner Ann Lippmann will be the city's liaison with the Tunnell-Spangler-Walsh team. According to Grindstaff, one of the reasons they picked TSW was their philosophy of development. "Their work rejects the formulaic development patterns of the last forty years in favor of the traditional principles of American town and city planning which shaped our communities prior to World War II. Union City is very much interested in recapturing that 'feel' right here and is greatly encouraged by TSW's feeling that we offer a real chance of achieving that result."

UNION CITY JOINS REGIONAL AUTHORITY

The South Fulton Municipal Regional Water and Sewer Authority, a joint effort between Union City, Fairburn, and Palmetto that was created in July 2000 with the purpose of constructing a reservoir that would supply water to the three growing cities, is becoming a reality. In November the Authority issued a $41.65-million bond to begin development. The Authority is negotiating to buy land in the southernmost part of the county for a 350-acre reservoir that would hold thirteen million gallons of water.

Mayors' Park

The ultimate goal of the Authority is to have greater control of water for the three cities, ending reliance on the City of Atlanta. In the upcoming weeks the Atlanta City Council is scheduled to vote on a rate increase to fund the $3.2-billion plan to repair and upgrade the city's sewer system. As a wholesale purchaser of water from Atlanta, those problems will be transferred to citizens of Union City.

Approval from the State Environmental Protection Division and the U.S. Army Corps of Engineers is necessary before construction can begin.

COMMUNITY COLLEGE COMES TO UNION CITY

On September 29, 2008, Georgia Military College Community College will begin classes at the Union City Community Activities Center. Based in Milledgeville, GMC Community College is accredited to award associate degrees in business administration, criminal justice, and general studies.

Tuition charges are fifty dollars per quarter hour. Twelve hours per quarter is considered full-time. Tuition assistance is available. The majority of students attending full-time paid only $267 for tuition in the spring quarter of 1998 after the Georgia Tuition Equalization Grant was applied. All tuition and fees are payable at the time of registration.

GMC also provides students with a book leasing program, which reduces the cost of books to approximately thirty-five dollars per course.

Regional Jail

City Hall

City Hall Marker

New City Hall, built in 1985

Union City Justice Center

Mayors' Park
with train.

New ladder fire truck
for Fire Station #3 in
Christian City.

Union City Police Department

Georgia Military College

Union Station, formerly called
Shannon Mall.

New Fire Station #1 on High Point Road

Mayors of Union City, Georgia

D. A. Carmical
1908–1913

J. O. Yarbrough
1913–1917

Walter Cowart
1917–1921

C. H. Gullatt
1921–1925

Ed Creel
1925–1929

Paul Barrett
1929–1935

Grady Cook
1935–1939

Bernard Yarbrough
1939–1943

Bill Hendrix
1943–1947

Elton Crowe
1947–1951

Raymond Burdett
1951–1955

Bernard Yarbrough
1955–1959

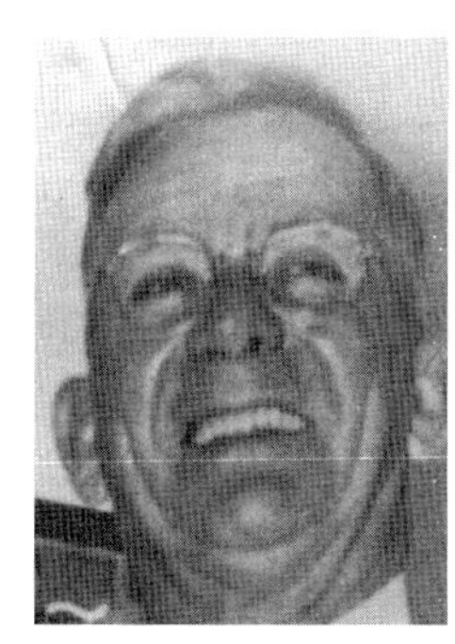
W. H. Y. Thornton
1959–1961

P. H. Houston
1961–1963

Elton Crowe
1963–1969

Harold Braswell
1969–1973

Bonny D. Adams
1973–1981

Fred Etris
1981–1993

Ralph Moore
1994–Present

ACKNOWLEDGMENTS

I would like to acknowledge all the individuals who worked tirelessly to make this publication possible. I would also like to ask forgiveness if I omit anyone whose contributions we greatly appreciated. So many of you gave us your family photos and stories, and for this we are very thankful.

Truly, this book would not be possible without the persistence of Patsy Williford. She and I were not so sure we could get enough photos to make this a book. Unlike me, Patsy is a native of this town and it was through her that we were able to gain access into the lives of so many people. She also helped to authenticate the information we gathered.

The same can be said for two other individuals whose connection to Union City complemented Patsy's. They are Sally Chapman and Mike Isome. Were it not for Sally, Patsy and I may have given up. Sally came in like the cavalry, armed with photos and stories to make this project a reality. Mike Isome gave us a glimpse into the African American experience in Union City. Mike not only provided the photos and the stories, he was history—Mike was the first African American police chief in Union City and his grandfather was the first police officer. Very special thanks to Joann Cummings and Nancy Martin, our resident photographers, for their contributions to this group. When asked to assist us, Joann and Nancy immediately set out to capture our town in photographs and interview those whose contributions we knew would be invaluable.

To the Union City Centennial Committee, I thank you for providing the incentive to take up this project. To the mayor, Ralph Moore, there were many days I could not have believed I said yes when you asked me to chair this committee, then to also publish this pictorial yearbook. There were many times Patsy and I thought it would not happen, but we were so fortunate to have met some wonderful people along the way.

Thanks to Mrs. Hamilton whose memory still amazes me, to Milton Foster, and to Mr. West for their invaluable background information. Mr. Louie Deaton came to our aid with not only a wealth of knowledge about the entire region but with photographs to match his stories. Thank you Mr. Deaton! A very special thanks to Dr. Robert and Jo Croom for their editing and their support for this project!

As with any worthwhile endeavor it has been a learning experience, one I will never forget and hopefully neither will you!

Marilyn Singleton McCain

CONTRIBUTORS

Barrett, Charles S., Barrett Biography in the American National Biography
Braswell, James Taylor
Bridges, Edith Elaine, Mrs.
Brown, Connie Whelchel
Bufffington, Ned
Carter, Sonja
Chapman, Sally Summers
Cochran, Mrs. Marion (Betty)
Cornell, Nancy Jones
Croom, Robert, Dr.
Croom, Jo
Cummings, Joann
Deaton, Louie F.
Drake, Vesta Gullatt, Early History of Union City
Fayette County Historical Society
Fields, Betty Jeanes
Foster, Milton
Green, A. J.
Greer, Fred
Hamilton, Lillie Belle Drake
Hartman, Edna (Missy) Yarbrough
Isome, Mike
Johnson, Linda
Lewis, W. J., Mrs.
Litoff, Judy Barrett, Dr.
McCain, Marilyn S.
Martin, Nancy
Mashburn, Odell
Melear, W. M., Family
Miller, Polly
Moore, Ralph, Mayor
Old Campbell County Historical Society
Potts, Robert
Reeves, Frances Cowart
Shinholster, Kathryn Yarbrough
Shadnor First Baptist Church
Turner, Helen
Union City, City of
West, Marcell
Williford, Patsy Moore
Yarbrough, B. A. Family

ABOUT THE AUTHORS AND CONTRIBUTORS

Marilyn Singleton McCain, MBA in healthcare management, has been a Union City resident since 1976 and has a thirty-year career in healthcare. She is currently employed as a healthcare manager at Grady Health System and was appointed to the Union City Planning Commission in 2001. She is chairperson of the Planning Commission, chair of the Union City Centennial Celebration Committee, American Red Cross Blood Drive coordinator, a member of the Olivet Church, president of the Shannon Glen Homeowners Association, a member of several civic organizations, and president of Lab Check, LLC, a healthcare consulting firm. A graduate of American Intercontinental University and Spelman College, she is the mother of one son, James Thomas McCain III.

Sally Summers Chapman is a native of Union City who attended Union City Elementary School and graduated from Campbell High School with a commercial course. Retired after a thirty-two-year career with the Federal Aviation Administration (FAA), she is a member of Shadnor First Baptist Church and the mother of two sons, Steven Patterson and James Farr, and two grandchildren, Stephanie and Scott Patterson. Currently a resident of nearby Senoia, Georgia, she still has a deep abiding love for Union City.

Patsy Williford is a native of Union City who attended Union City Elementary School and graduated from Campbell High School. She is married to W. H. (Sonny) Williford, Jr., a business owner in Union City. She is the mother of two children and has two grandsons. She is retired from Union City after seventeen years of service.

Joann Cummings—A native Atlantan and a graduate of Morris Brown College in Atlanta, she moved to Union City in 1986 with her husband Charles and daughter Tracie. She is retired from AT&T, active in College Park Methodist Church and the Washington High School alumni association, a volunteer with Fulton County voter registration, a member of the Union City Housing Authority, a Grady Health System Blood Drive volunteer, and a Union City Senior Citizen League volunteer.

Louie Deaton is a resident of Fairburn, Georgia, and is retired from the Forestry Commission. He was Georgia's first unit forester in charge of forest fires, forest management, and forest public education in Fulton County. He is also Georgia's first urban forester. He did the Smokey Bear programs, Fourth of July parades for WSB-TV, forestry programs for TV and radio in the Atlanta area, and forestry dioramas across the state of Georgia. His area of responsibility included Union City, Fairburn, Palmetto, College Park, East Point, and southwest Atlanta. He is the recipient of the governor's award for outstanding service.

Mike Isome is a native of Union City and recently retired chief of police. He is a graduate of Northwood University in Michigan. Mike was also the first African American police chief for the city. Mike is married to Bridgette Isome and together they have four children and seven grandchildren.

Nancy Martin is a native of Atlanta and a resident of Union City since December 1988. She graduated from Clark-Atlanta University and has worked twenty-four years with the United States Environmental Protection Agency. She is currently senior budget analyst in the budget operations section as well as vice president of the Wellington Estates Homeowners Association and mother of Delrico Juwon Harshaw.

808
CENTRAL OF GEORGIA
DUFFEEHOUSE
DUFFEE
HOTEL
452